FIRST ST[ ]
IN
FAMILY HISTORY

Anthony J Camp

1998

Published by

Society of Genealogists
14 Charterhouse Buildings
Goswell Road
London EC1M 7BA

Registered Charity No. 233701

First published 1993
Second edition 1995
Third edition 1998

© Society of Genealogists 1998

ISBN 1 85951 088 4

British Library Cataloguing in Publication Data

A CIP Catalogue record for this book is available from the British Library

CONTENTS

1
BEGINNING THE SEARCH

Searching for your ancestors must begin with what you know about yourself, your parents and grandparents. That is the first rule: you work from the known to the unknown. Collect all the family documents you can and question your relatives. The older ones may know about letters, diaries, papers and dated photographs. They may be able to estimate ages and suggest locations, even if they cannot give the exact details of dates and places of births, marriages and deaths which you will need to add in due course. If you are lucky there may be birthday books or even a Family Bible containing vital dates. It is not only the dates and places which are important. Information about occupation and physical characteristics as well as family life and anecdotes should also be collected.

The source of every fact you are told or which you find in documents and books should be carefully noted. Sooner or later you will find that the information you are collecting does not always agree and you will need to be able to check back to see which source is likely to be more accurate. You will find that even a source like a Family Bible may not always be relied upon, with entries being added years after the event and dates of birth calculated incorrectly from estimated ages at death.

Remember that when you ask older people about the family no person will tell you everything that he or she knows at one sitting or in one letter. You may need to go back several times, to trigger reminiscences with old photographs and to discuss the finds in your continuing research, when 'new' names or details may unlock further memories. Do not neglect approaching younger children or cousins who may have nursed aged parents or grandparents and inherited their personal possessions. Remember that members of the family who do not appear helpful or interested may be glad to point out errors when you circulate a draft pedigree of what you have found. Never overlook cousins overseas who may have cherished family letters and photographs as links with 'home' long after copies in Britain have been destroyed.

Sometimes the vaguest of remarks may prove unexpectedly useful at a later stage and every comment should be noted, together with its source and the date on which the information was given. As with printed information, family stories do not always contain an element of truth, however, and everything should be approached with an open mind until clear proof is forthcoming.

2
RECORD THE INFORMATION AS YOU GO

It is important when you begin not to trace too many lines of ancestry at the same time, else it is very easy to get overwhelmed in detail. Most people trace the male line because that is usually the surname they bear, but there is no reason why you should not trace your mother's family or some other line of ancestry if you wish.

It is equally important to record what you learn about each relative on a separate card or better still on the page of a loose-leaf notebook as you proceed. When taking extracts from written sources keep the notes from each source separate and keep material on one family quite separate from that on another.

It will not be possible to put everything you discover on a pedigree chart but you may find it helpful to summarise the main details on a 'drop-line chart pedigree' so that the relationships of the various members of the family one to another are clear. Such a chart should show full names and occupations, and the dates and places of birth and/or baptism, marriage and death and/or burial.

Dates should always be expressed as 11 November 1911 or 1911 November 11 and not as 11.11.11. There is then no possibility of confusion between the day and the month, let alone of the century.

Always date every pedigree which you compile so that you can see which one contains the latest state of your knowledge. Photocopies of such charts, neatly written or typed, can be made cheaply and should be circulated to other members of the family as the search develops. If these charts are slightly reduced in the photocopying any background guide lines or joins in the paper will conveniently disappear.

If you are not very methodical in your work then you may find printed form 'family group sheets' and 'pedigree charts' helpful. These show immediately what is known about each family group, though they leave little space for recording other details and the sources used. A variety of forms and charts may be seen in the bookshop at the Society of Genealogists (see Section 12) and others are available from LBS Ancestral Records, Freepost 691, Herne Bay, Kent CT6 8BR (tel. 01227 375776) and Allen & Todd, 9-11 Square Street, Ramsbottom, Lancashire BL0 9JD (tel. 01706 827988).

If you begin to find a lot of information about each person then it is important to start writing a narrative account of the family as soon as possible. If you leave this until your searches are completed it may never get done! The account, which should include your own personal reminiscences about yourself and other members of your family, can be illustrated with copies of photographs and postcard views of ancestral places. It then begins to form a permanent and valuable record for the family which is easily understood and appreciated by all its members. Several firms which specialise in copying photographs and which sell postcard views advertise in the monthly *Family Tree Magazine* (available on some bookstalls or from 61 Great Whyte, Ramsey, Huntingdon, Cambridgeshire PE17 1HL; tel. 01487 814050).

3
DEVELOPING YOUR KNOWLEDGE

The further back you get, the more scanty family information will become in most if not all lines. Therefore, while you are visiting older members of the family it will be necessary for you to read about the next steps.

Of the many books of advice, the following can be recommended: Andrew Todd, *Basic sources for family history: back to the early 1800s* (Allen & Todd, Ramsbottom, 3rd edn. 1994, 96 pages; £4.00); Jean Cole and John Titford, *Tracing your family tree* (Countryside Books, Newbury, 1997, 256 pages; £9.95) and M.D. Herber, *Ancestral trails: the complete guide to to British genealogy and family history* (Sutton Publishing, Stroud, 1997, 674 pages; £30.00).

For those with Irish, Scottish and Welsh ancestry the following books can be recommended: T. McCarthy, *The Irish roots guide* (Lilliput, Dublin, 1991, 116 pages; £4.99) and J. Grenham, *Tracing your Irish ancestors: the complete guide* (Gill and Macmillan, Dublin, 1992, 319 pages; £10.99); K.B. Cory, *Tracing your Scottish ancestry* (Polygon, Edinburgh, 2nd edn. 1997, 212 pages; £7.95); John Rowlands and others, *Welsh family history: a guide to research* (Federation of Family History Societies, 2nd edn. due 1998).

If you find reference to some source of information which you do not fully understand then Terrick FitzHugh, *The dictionary of genealogy* (A & C Black, London, 4th edn. 1994; £21.99) or P. Saul, *The family historian's enquire within*

(Federation of Family History Societies, 5th edn. with amendments 1997; £9.50) may be helpful.

4
IS SOMEBODY ELSE WORKING ON THIS FAMILY?

As there are many thousands of people throughout the world who are tracing their ancestors it is as well to see if there is anyone else working on the same line as yourself. An enormous number of families in which people are interested have been listed in various commercial directories and these should not on any account be overlooked. Check as many as you can; duplication of effort is wasteful, but sharing research with relatives can be of great benefit to both parties.

Many people advertised the surnames on which they were working in the *National genealogical directory* which was published annually between 1979 and 1993 (originally by M.J. Burchall and latterly by I. Caley). Many more entries appear in the *Genealogical research directory* (ed. by K.A. Johnson & M.R. Sainty, Library of Australian History, Sydney) which has been published annually since 1981 and is widely available. Each issue contains at least a hundred thousand entries. Those who advertise their interests in one issue, however, may not do so in the next and it is worthwhile to check as many editions as possible. The *Genealogical research directory*, which relates to families being researched all over the world, also contains the addresses and other details of most family history societies worldwide.

Many local family history societies (see below, Section 14) have published lists of their members' 'interests' and other searchers publish their interests in the monthly *Family Tree Magazine* mentioned above. The Society of Genealogists (see below, Section 12) maintains a card index of its own 'Members' Interests'.

The largest single index of this kind is the *British Isles genealogical register* ('BIG-R') which lists families being researched in the United Kingdom only. The first edition, published by the Federation of Family History Societies on microfiche in 1994, contained over 300,000 entries, and a second edition with 219,740 entries appeared in 1997. They should not on any account be overlooked.

5
HAS IT BEEN DONE BEFORE?

If a family history has already been researched and published in book form you will find a reference to it in T.R. Thomson, *Catalogue of British family histories* (3rd edn., London, 1980).

Accounts of families are to be found in many local and county histories, biographical studies, national and local periodicals, transactions of archaeological and record societies, and in a multitude of out-of-the-way and forgotten books. In the last century, Dr G.W. Marshall went through works of this nature making notes of every tabular pedigree or account of a family that he came across which gave at least three generations in the male line. These are all listed in his *The genealogist's guide* (4th edn. 1903; reprinted London & Baltimore, 1967).

Marshall's *Guide* will give you references to most pedigrees printed before 1903, but some of those he missed and most of those published in the first fifty years of this century were indexed by Major J.B. Whitmore in *A genealogical guide* (London, 1953).

Continuing Whitmore's work, G.B. Barrow published another volume also called *The genealogist's guide* (London & Chicago, 1977) listing family history material which was published in the next twenty-five years.

Together, these three books - and you must consult all three - list most material printed on any family in England, and they are quite indispensable. If you want to come a little more up to date, you will find in the back of Thomson's *Catalogue* mentioned above an Appendix of family histories printed between 1975 and 1980 which is the only compilation of its kind for this period.

These authors made no particular search for Scottish and Irish material. For printed pedigrees of Scottish families you will need to consult M. Stuart, *Scottish family history* (Edinburgh, 1930), which is brought up to date by J.P.S. Ferguson, *Scottish family histories* (Edinburgh, 2nd edn. 1986). The latter lists in addition those Scottish libraries known to possess copies. Both should be consulted.

For Irish printed pedigrees there are two books: B. de Breffny, *Bibliography of Irish family history and genealogy* (Cork, 1974) and the more up-to-date

E. MacLysaght, *Bibliography of Irish family history* (Dublin, 1982). Both should be consulted.

Your public library will probably not have all the books and periodicals mentioned in these bibliographies and it may not be easy to find copies of particular items. Many will be found at the Society of Genealogists (see below, Section 12). If you go to the Society for the bibliographies you will find them on the Textbook Shelves in the Middle Library.

If there is nothing in print, the Society may have a typescript or manuscript family history. You will need to consult the Family History section of the Library Catalogue. That will tell you if there is any bound material.

Unbound material is kept in the Document Collection in the Upper Library where there are files on many thousands of families in alphabetical order. Material received since 1992 has been microfiched and the fiche are available in the Lower Library. After that, you should return to the Upper Library and look at the card index of pedigrees in deposited and other special collections.

The Society of Genealogists is always glad to add any pedigree to its collection and its receipt will automatically be mentioned in the *Genealogists' magazine*. If your donation includes your address, this is an effective method of getting in touch with other people interested in the same surname, both now and in the future.

If the family has an hereditary right to a coat of arms you may find that a pedigree has been registered at the College of Arms, Queen Victoria Street, London EC4V 4BT (tel. 0171 248 2762). No list of the pedigrees registered there has been printed. However, a pedigree may have been registered at the College at the time of a grant of arms and an index of many grants of arms before 1898 is to be found in *Grantees of arms before 1898* (Harleian Society, vols. 66-68, London, 1915-17).

A pedigree may also have been given to the local family history society of the area to which it relates (see Section 14) or to the appropriate county record office (see Section 13).

As mentioned above many family history societies have published lists of the families on which their members are working, and articles about their research may also appear in their magazines. A card index of articles on families and other matters which have appeared in local family history society magazines since 1976 is maintained at the Society of Genealogists.

As your search develops and you go further back in time and find perhaps that your ancestors have moved from one county to another you will need to consult these various indexes again. References which seemed irrelevant when you commenced your work may later suddenly acquire greater relevance.

Remember, however, that a published or manuscript pedigree is not necessarily either complete or accurate. Its accuracy can only be judged by the extent to which it quotes the authorities on which it has been based. You may, therefore, need to check it carefully against parish registers, wills and other original documents.

Another warning needs repeating here. Because a family of the same surname has been traced in the past, even in the same locality, that does not mean that there is necessarily a relationship. Concentrate on your own immediate family and work steadily back on that; resist all temptation to work down from some presumed ancestor with the same surname. That is a sure way of tracing other people's ancestors.

6
ONE-NAME STUDIES, FAMILY ASSOCIATIONS AND CLANS

Some genealogists trace everyone with a particular surname and, if they are willing to share and exchange information about it, they may belong to the Guild of One-Name Studies or 'GOONS' (Box G, 14 Charterhouse Buildings, Goswell Road, London EC1M 7BA). The Guild has about 1,000 members and a list of the families on which they are working is given in the Guild's *Register of one-name studies* which is published annually (GOONS, 13th edn. 1997; £3.95). Other 'one-name' searchers are listed in the *Genealogical research directory* and in the *British Isles genealogical register*.

There are also many family associations worldwide. Those which published some kind of periodical or newsletter were listed in I.J. Marker & K.E. Warth, *Surname periodicals: a world-wide listing of one-name genealogical publications* (GOONS, 1987). Others appear in E.P. Bentley, *Directory of family associations* (Baltimore, USA, 3rd edn. 1996).

A list of the Chiefs of Clans and Names in Scotland, with their addresses, is published annually in *Whitaker's Almanack* and a list of the family surname organisations which have been dubbed 'Clans of Ireland' can be obtained from the Clans of Ireland Office, 2 Kildare Street, Dublin 2.

With all this activity you may think that there is little left to be done, but the great majority of people tracing their ancestors find that the work they are doing, at least in the early stages, is unique and has not been done before. After that there is quite likely to be an overlap with someone somewhere. If you deposit copies of the fruits of your labours at the Society of Genealogists as soon as you can, you are likely to make contacts and discover long-lost cousins much sooner than you think.

7
CIVIL REGISTRATION

From the above-mentioned publications you will learn that for births, marriages and deaths in England and Wales since 1 July 1837, details of names, dates, ages, addresses and occupations can be obtained by purchasing certificates at the Family Records Centre, 1 Myddelton Street, London EC1R 1UW (tel. 0181 392 5300; open Monday, Wednesday & Friday 9.00-5.00, Tuesday 10.00-7.00, Thursday 9.00-7.00 & Saturday 9.30-5.00).

Here, on the ground floor and in a section of the building run by the General Register Office, you may search the quarterly indexes of births, marriages and deaths without charge. Before 1911 these merely show the name of the person registered and the place of registration, though the deaths indexes include the stated age at death from 1866 onwards. Their value, however, lies in the fact that they cover all England and Wales in one alphabetical series.

The full biographical detail and connecting information is only available if you purchase a certificate. Each certificate costs £6.50 and takes four days to prepare. You may wish to collect it and then carry out the next stage of the search, or you can have it posted without further charge. If there is more than one likely entry in the indexes for the event you require you may ask for each to be checked against a known fact (e.g. exact date of birth or name of father). If an entry does not agree with the facts you have given, then £3 is returned to you.

About two thousand people a day use these indexes and it is advisable to avoid the crush in the search room particularly at lunchtime by going on a Monday or Friday or for the first hour in the morning. Overcoats and bags should be left in the lockers in the basement (operated with a £1 coin which is refunded) and bored family members in the refreshment room there. If you cannot go yourself you will find advertisements of many searchers who offer special rates for work there in *Family Tree Magazine* (details at end of Section 2, above).

The usual manner of working is to search for a known birth, such as that of your father or grandfather, and then with the information on that birth certificate to search for the marriage of his parents, working backwards from the date of birth until the marriage is found (each party having the same reference in the indexes). The marriage certificate will normally give an indication of the age of the parties so that their births can be searched for and the process repeated.

Of course one's exact age at any time was less important in the past than it is now. Ages on death certificates are frequently incorrect and those on marriage certificates should always be treated with caution. They may have been increased or lowered for a variety of reasons.

Copies of the indexes are available in some libraries on microfilm or microfiche and there is a set at the Society of Genealogists from 1837 to 1920. Certificates may be obtained by post from the General Register Office, Postal Applications Section, Smedley Hydro, Trafalgar Road, Birkdale, Southport PR8 2HH (tel. 0151 471 4200), but cost £13 (air mail) or £12 (surface mail) unless the exact reference from the indexes is known, when the charge is £9.

A birth or death taking place at the end of one quarter may be registered and appear in the indexes for the next quarter. Registration of births was far from complete in the early years of civil registration and occasionally the indexes themselves are an approach should be made to the local Registrar of Births and he or she may then be able to identify the entry. An unregistered child may in any case have been baptised and appear in the appropriate church registers. A very large number of baptisms between 1837 and 1875 are to be found on the International Genealogical Index (see below, Section 10). It was quite easy to give an illegitimate child a legitimate birth certificate and if the marriage of the parents of a child cannot be found then it is useful to assume that one of the parents is already married to someone else and to search for that marriage.

Other reasons for the apparent non-registration of a birth or marriage are that variations in the forenames and even of the surname itself have not been taken into account. Many people in the last century assumed additional forenames at marriage or in later life. Many others prior to the introduction of basic elementary education in the 1870s had no conception of a 'correct' spelling for their surname and the sound which they made when repeating it might well be transmitted to paper in different ways by different people. This is an important point to bear in mind the further back you go, and you should always be on the look out for possible variations of the surname you are researching.

Events in Scotland

For such events in Scotland from 1855, apply to the Search Unit, New Register House, Edinburgh EH1 3YT (open Monday-Thursday 9.00-4.30, Friday 9.00-4.00). Computerised indexes from 1855 to date may be consulted for an half-hourly charge of £4 on the ground floor of the Family Records Centre, London, as part of 'Scotlink', but prior booking is essential. The indexes are also available on microfilm, 1855-1920 only, at the Society of Genealogists.

Events in Ireland

The address for Northern Ireland events from 1922 is General Register Office, Oxford House, 49-55 Chichester Street, Belfast BT1 4HL. Earlier certificates and those for the rest of Ireland from 1864 (with non-Catholic marriages from 1845) can be obtained from the General Register Office, 8-11 Lombard Street East, Dublin 2.

Events overseas and in the army

Also at the Family Records Centre, 1 Myddelton Street, London EC1R 1UW, are various indexes to events overseas and in the army. The chief ones are:

Consular Returns: births, marriages and deaths of British subjects overseas 1849-1965.

Marine Register: births and deaths at sea 1837-1965.

Regimental Returns: births in the United Kingdom and overseas 1761-1924. The overseas returns start about 1790.

Army Chaplains' Returns: overseas births, marriages and deaths 1796-1965.

War Deaths: Natal and South Africa Forces 1899-1902, First World War 1914-21, Second World War 1939-1948.

Because many of these overseas and army records duplicate and overlap with records held elsewhere (in the Public Record Office and the Guildhall Library) it is wise to read the section on 'Births, marriages and deaths of Britons overseas' in A. Bevan and A. Duncan, *Tracing your ancestors in the Public Record Office* (HMSO, 4th edn. 4th impression, 1995; £7.95) before purchasing certificates. This supplements the valuable country by country survey in *The British overseas: a guide to records of their births, baptisms, marriages, deaths and burials, available in the United Kingdom* (Guildhall Library, 3rd edn. 1994; £5.75) but its general introductory pages must also be consulted.

Events in India

Perhaps one should add here that the records of births, marriages and deaths in India, with indexes, from 1698 to 1948, originally returned to the East India Company, are now at the British Library, Oriental & India Office Collections, 197 Blackfriars Road, London SE1 8NG (tel. 0171 412 7873). These Collections are due to be transferred to the new British Library building at St Pancras in August 1998.

8
CENSUS RETURNS 1841-1891

Once you know the locations of some relatives a hundred or more years ago, you can consult the official census returns for 1891, 1881, 1871, 1861 and 1851, which record street by street the members of each household, their relationship to its head, ages, occupations and birthplaces. The 1841 census is also available, but does not show relationships or places of birth.

A complete set of the census returns for England, Wales, the Isle of Man and the Channel Islands can be seen without charge on microfilm on the first floor at the Family Records Centre (see Section 7), in a section of the building run by the Public Record Office. No reader's ticket is needed to consult the census returns. Here there are street indexes for the larger towns and a good collection of surname indexes. First time visitors may care to read S. Lumas, *Making use of the census* (PRO, 1997; £5.99), which explains the procedures in a helpful way.

Microfilms of census returns for particular counties are often held by county record offices (see Section 13) and city libraries and many have been indexed by surname by local family history societies. For the available indexes see J. Gibson & E. Hampson, *Marriage, census and other indexes for family historians* (Federation of Family History Societies, 6th edn. 1996; £3.50).

Of great assistance are the detailed indexes and transcriptions of the 1881 census returns for the whole of England, Scotland, Wales, the Channel Islands and the Isle of Man, compiled by the Genealogical Society of Utah. These county indexes are widely available on microfiche and consolidated CD-ROM versions for each country are intended. An index of those on board Royal Navy ships that year is also available.

Large collections of census indexes for other years are also to be found at the Society of Genealogists (see Section 12) and the Public Record Office (see Section 15).

People do not always know or tell the truth about their ages and places of birth and it is wise to search all the available census returns for possible variant information as well as for additional members of the family. The ages and places of birth of the parents of a child born in 1890 may, for instance, be found from the 1891 census returns and then similar details of the grandparents found from the 1871 returns of these places of birth (or perhaps more easily from the indexed 1881 returns), with perhaps the great-grandparents being found in the same way in 1851. Even the ages and places of birth of the parents of a person who was born about 1815 and who married in 1840 may still be discovered from the 1851 returns if they survived to that date.

The Scottish census returns 1841-1891, arranged by parish, are available at New Register House, Princes Street, Edinburgh EH1 3YT, where a fee is charged. The 1881 indexes mentioned above are available on microfiche and a simple surname index to the 1891 returns has also been published on microfiche. The 1891 index is available on computer at the Family Records Centre, London, as part of 'Scotlink' (see above, Section 7). The first complete Irish census extant is that for 1901, which, with that for 1911, can be seen at the National Archives of Ireland, Bishop Street, Dublin 8, Eire. It is arranged by townland or, in urban areas, by street.

9

WILLS AND ADMINISTRATIONS

Much useful information can be gleaned from wills and administrations, copies of which for England and Wales back to 1858 may be seen (£0.25 each) and photocopies obtained (£0.75 each) at the Principal Registry of the Family Division, Somerset House, Strand, London WC2R 1LP (tel. 0171 936 7000; open Monday-Friday, 10.00-4.30). No reader's ticket or appointment is required. Documents may take an hour to be produced. The public search room is due to be moved to First Avenue House, High Holborn in June 1998.

For those with something to bequeath, the annual will indexes on the open shelves here are more informative than death certificates. They show date and place of death as well as the names (and, in early years, relationships) of the executors. From 1858 to 1870 the wills and administrations are indexed separately but from 1871 onwards they are indexed together in annual volumes covering all England and Wales. Wills of people dying overseas but with property in England or Wales also appear.

The indexes are easier and quicker to use than the General Register Office death indexes at the Family Records Centre and if you are searching over a long period or cannot find the death entries you require, a search here is recommended. In cases where the surname is very frequent the will indexes may be used to eliminate possible entries found in the death indexes.

There are copies of the indexes of wills and administrations in some major libraries and District Probate Registries. There is a set on microfiche 1858-1943 at the Family Records Centre (see above, Section 7) and there are microfilm copies 1858-1930, re-organised by the initial letter of the surname, at the Society of Genealogists (see below, Section 12).

Prior to 1858 a will was proved in one of the three hundred local church courts depending on where the deceased's personal property was located. The Family Records Centre (see above, Section 7) holds records 1383-1858 of the Prerogative Court of Canterbury, the senior probate court in England and Wales, with many wills for London and the south-east of England. Fully alphabetical indexes are available there for the period 1383-1800 and 1853-58 otherwise the manuscript calendars must be searched. Here also are the Estate Duty Office Registers 1796-1858 which contain abstracts of most wills in England and Wales 1815-1858.

Wills proved in the subsidiary church courts before 1858 are usually to be found in the appropriate county record offices (see below, Section 13). The Society of Genealogists (see below, Section 12) holds copy indexes for many of them.

10
PARISH REGISTERS

Before civil registration started (1837 in England and Wales, 1855 in Scotland, and 1864 in Ireland) births and deaths were not recorded as such, but baptisms, marriages and burials were entered in the registers of the appropriate churches or chapels.

Some parish, or Church of England, registers date from 1538. Most of those over a hundred years old are now deposited in county record offices and only a very few remain in parish churches. Access to original registers in public hands is mostly free; for those at the church the clergy are allowed to make a charge (from 1 January 1998: £12 for the first hour and £10 for each subsequent hour or part of an hour).

The whereabouts of any register may be determined from C.R. Humphery-Smith, *The Phillimore atlas and index of parish registers* (Phillimore, 2nd edn. 1995; £50) and the addresses and opening hours of the record offices mentioned are shown in *Record repositories in Great Britain* (PRO Publications, 10th edn. 1997; £3.99).

Over the years a great many parish registers have been copied and indexed, often to 1812 (when the form of the baptismal and burial registers changed and printed columns were introduced) or to 1837 or later. Many more have been microfilmed by the Genealogical Society of Utah. The largest collection of these copies in the British Isles is at the Society of Genealogists. The places and years covered are given in *Parish register copies in the library of the Society of Genealogists* (Society of Genealogists, 11th edn. 1995; £5.95).

From the various available copies three important centralised indexes have been compiled:

(1) **International Genealogical Index**: this contains about eighty million baptisms and marriages from parish registers between 1538 and 1875. They are arranged in alphabetical order of surname and forename in county sections. Variations in the surnames have been brought together but abbreviated and Latinised forms of forenames have not. The dates are those of baptism not of birth. This index, compiled by the Genealogical Society of Utah is known as the International Genealogical Index (or I.G.I.). Several editions have been produced on microfiche (the most recent in 1992) and it is widely available in county record offices, libraries and Family History Centres (see below, Section 16). At some centres the 1988 or 1992 edition with its addenda can be consulted on computers where it forms part of a group of programs known as FamilySearch. The computerised version allows country-wide searches to be made for a particular baptism or marriage, or, in a 'parent search', for the children born to a marriage. A full set of the I.G.I. includes material from every country worldwide as well as events at sea and contains altogether about 240 million entries of baptism and marriage. An indication of the parishes and periods covered is provided by the microfiche 'Parish and vital records list' but it should be used with care.

(2) **Boyd's Marriage Index**: this contains about seven million marriages in England between 1538 and 1837, arranged in alphabetical order of surname and forename in 25-year sections, divided by county, in 531 volumes. The 3,000 parishes and periods covered are listed in *A list of parishes in Boyd's Marriage Index* (Society of Genealogists, 6th edn. 1994; £3.25). There is a typescript copy of the Index at the Society of Genealogists and microfiche copies are available at many Family History Centres.

(3) **Pallot's Marriage Index**: covers most marriages in the London area 1780-1837. It is arranged in alphabetical order in one sequence on paper slips, but no copies are available and postal searches only are possible. Apply to Achievements Ltd., 79-82 Northgate, Canterbury, Kent CT1 1BA. Fees are payable; the minimum charge being £15.

Other county marriage and burial indexes are being compiled by local family history societies and individuals. Several counties are completely covered. Although not normally accessible for personal searches these indexes may usually be searched for quite small fees. They are listed with the fees involved in J. Gibson & E. Hampson, *Marriage, census and other indexes for family historians* (Federation of Family History Societies, 6th edn. 1996; £3.50).

It cannot be too strongly stressed that in each and every case where entries are found in indexes of this kind they should be checked and the full details obtained from the original registers themselves. The main indexes are not complete and no conclusions should be drawn solely from the evidence which they contain. The original registers of the places from which your ancestors came should always be searched over wide periods and the burial registers should never be neglected. Each ancestor's death or burial should always be sought out and recorded before you proceed to search back for details of the earlier generation. The age at death may indicate an approximate date of birth. If the death of a widow cannot be found remember that she may have re-married and changed her name.

It is unfortunate that the register entries themselves are frequently very uninformative but they must still be looked at. A baptism will normally give the forenames of both parents (but not the maiden name of the mother). A marriage before 1837 will usually only show the names of the parties involved and not their ages or the names of their parents (though the names of the two witnesses recorded after 1754 may be useful). And a burial before 1813 will only show the age of the deceased if one is comparatively lucky. Occupations only rarely appear.

Useful summary lists of English and Welsh parishes, showing the whereabouts of their parish registers, the availability of copies and the extent to which they are covered by the above indexes, are published in C.R. Humphery-Smith, *The Phillimore atlas and index of parish registers* (Phillimore, 2nd edn. 1995; £50).

Scottish parish registers

Most Scottish parish registers before 1855 are at New Register House, Princes Street, Edinburgh EH1 3YT. Few begin before 1750 but all the baptisms and marriages (but not the burials) prior to 1855 have been indexed by the Genealogical Society of Utah. The indexes to these 'Old Parochial Registers' are arranged by county and are available on microfiche at various libraries and Family History Centres. There is a set at the Society of Genealogists. They are also available as part of 'Scotlink' at the Family Records Centre (see above, Section 7).

Welsh parish registers

The above comments about English registers generally apply, but for the whereabouts of Welsh parish registers see C.J. Williams & J. Watts-Williams, *Parish registers of Wales* (Society of Genealogists, National Index of Parish Registers, vol. 13, 1986).

Irish parish registers

Many Irish registers have not survived. In the rural areas those which have survived date only from the early nineteenth century. In the Republic of Ireland the Church of Ireland registers before 1870 are Public Records. Most are still held by the local clergy, but some have been deposited in the National Archives of Ireland and others are at the Representative Church Body Library, Braemor Park, Rathgar, Dublin 14. Catholic parish registers are normally still held by the parish priest, but there are microfilms of most prior to 1880 in the National Archives, Bishop Street, Dublin 8. Records from parishes in Northern Ireland, which are not retained in parish custody, are deposited in the Public Record Office of Northern Ireland, 66 Balmoral Avenue, Belfast BT9 6NY. See Brian Mitchell, *Guide to Irish parish registers* (Baltimore, 1988).

11
NONCONFORMIST REGISTERS

If the family did not attend the Church of England its baptisms may be found in the registers of a nonconformist chapel. Few families remained staunchly Anglican and if expected events cannot be found in the Church of England registers then nonconformity should always be considered. Most surviving nonconformist registers in England and Wales before 1837 are at the Family Records Centre (see above, Section 7), but others remain in the various chapels or are deposited with the denominational headquarters or at the appropriate county record office.

The baptisms in the registers at the Family Records Centre have been indexed into the International Genealogical Index. Three important groups of nonconformist registers deposited at the Public Record Office, however, are not yet included in that Index. They are (1) the births and marriages of Quakers 1650s-1837, (2) the births and baptisms of Baptists, Congregationalists and Presbyterians registered at Dr Williams's Library 1743-1837, and (3) the births and baptisms of Wesleyans registered at the Wesleyan Metropolitan Registry 1818-1841.

Few nonconformist marriages, other than of Quakers and Jews, took place in England and Wales before 1837, and the marriages of Baptists, Catholics, Congregationalists, Methodists and English Presbyterians between 1754 and 1837 are normally found in Church of England registers. Catholics may, however, also have gone through private ceremonies which may have been recorded separately by the priests involved.

Some Catholic registers before 1837 are at the Family Records Centre (and are included in the I.G.I.) but others remain in the churches or have been deposited in local record offices. See M.J. Gandy, *Catholic missions and registers 1700-1880* (1993, 6 parts, each £6), which gives details of all known registers in England, Wales, Scotland, the Channel Islands and the Isle of Man.

Research back to 1837 should basically be carried out through the normal records of civil registration and the census returns. Once you have arrived at that date there are several volumes in the *My ancestors* series published by the Society of Genealogists which will be helpful: G.R. Breed, *My ancestors were Baptists* (3rd edn. 1995; £4.99); D.J.H. Clifford, *My ancestors were Congregationalists* (2nd edn. 1997; £3.90); I. Mordy, *My ancestors were Jewish* (2nd edn. 1995, £1.80); W. Leary, *My ancestors were Methodists* (2nd edn. 1990); A. Ruston, *My ancestors were English Presbyterians/Unitarians* (1993; £3) and E.H. Milligan & M.J. Thomas, *My ancestors were Quakers* (1983).

The surviving nonconformist registers of Wales are listed in D. Ifans, *Nonconformist registers of Wales* (1994; £14.50).

12
SOCIETY OF GENEALOGISTS

At this stage of your research it will be worth your while to visit the Society of Genealogists at 14 Charterhouse Buildings, Goswell Road, London EC1M 7BA (tel. 0171 251 8799; open Tuesday, Friday, Saturday, 10.00-6.00; Wednesday & Thursday 10.00-8.00).

You need not be a member of the Society as the library is open to searchers at a minimum charge of £3 for one hour, £7.50 for four hours or £10 for the day. No appointment is necessary. If you wish to stay all day there is a common room with a drinks machine for those bringing sandwiches.

If you join you also benefit from the quarterly *Genealogists' magazine*, discounts on the Society's publications, on lectures and seminars and on the courses for beginners, and days on which new members are taken round the Library and shown its resources. Members in the British Isles may also borrow printed books, microfilms and microfiche with certain exceptions. The membership fee is £30 a year and there is in addition an entrance fee of £7.50 payable on first joining.

An outline guide, *Using the library of the Society of Genealogists* (Society of Genealogists, 1997; £0.70) is available and should be read in advance by all visitors. The library, which was started in 1911 and has over 70,000 volumes as well as much manuscript and microform material, is arranged on three floors:

(a) **Middle Library: or British Isles Collection**: here on the first floor the shelves are arranged in alphabetical order of the old English counties from Bedfordshire to Yorkshire, followed by Scotland, Wales, Ireland, the Isle of Man and the Channel Islands. The books in each section are divided into eight groups:

(1) General works about the area and its records, such as bibliographies, histories, maps, newspapers, place names, record office guides, heralds' visitations and wills. For some areas there are large manuscript collections and indexes compiled by previous genealogists. These include Snell's Berkshire Collection, Rogers' Cornish Pedigrees, Boyd's Citizens of London and the Welply Collection of Irish will abstracts. The Macleod Collection for Scotland is on the floor above.

(2) Local histories and other topographical material, parish histories and church guides.

(3) Parish Registers. The Society has the largest collection of copies of parish registers in the country (about 8,000), including an almost complete series of all that have ever been printed and hundreds in typescript and manuscript. The parishes and dates covered (the earliest being 1538 and the latest generally 1837 though some may continue into this century) are listed in *Parish register copies in the library of the Society of Genealogists* (11th edn. 1995; £5.95). The collection and the published catalogue include over 600 nonconformist registers. There is full coverage for Scotland before 1855 and much Isle of Man and Guernsey material.

(4) Monumental inscriptions. The inscriptions on the tombstones in a large number of churchyards have been copied. There is a published catalogue, *Monumental inscriptions in the library of the Society of Genealogists* (2 vols. 1984 & 1987). Tombstone inscriptions (though

not always accurate, particularly where ages are concerned) are one of the most obvious sources of genealogical information. Many local family history societies have made great efforts to record all the inscriptions in their areas and county record offices may have copies of others which no longer survive made by antiquaries in the past.

(5) Censuses. The Society does not hold full copies of the Census Returns 1841-91 though there is complete coverage in 1881 and some counties are covered in other years, but it has a large collection of indexes to the names in them. There is a published catalogue, *Census copies and indexes in the library of the Society of Genealogists* (3rd edn. 1995; £4.95).

(6) Lists. These are lists of people living in the county at different times. They are mostly poll books and trade directories. Poll books show the names of those who voted in parliamentary elections between 1694 and 1832. Trade directories for many provincial towns have been published regularly from the 1770s and may contain alphabetical, classified and street lists. Similar national and county directories exist from the 1780s and grow in detail from the 1840s. There is a published catalogue, *Directories and poll books in the library of the Society of Genealogists* (6th edn. 1995; £7.60).

(7) Periodicals. These are the publications of the local record and archaeological societies and of all the local family history societies in the British Isles.

There is a published catalogue of the whole of the Scottish (1996) and Irish (1990) collections, and basic lists have been published for Lancashire (1990), Nottinghamshire (1989) and Surrey (1994).

(b) **Upper Library**: in this room on the second floor the main collections are:

(1) Document Collection. The large Collection contains miscellaneous manuscripts (pedigrees, will abstracts, notes and letters) donated by members and others, and is arranged by surname and place name. Material received since February 1992 has been microfiched and the fiche are available in the Lower Library.

(2) Family Histories. An extensive collection of printed, typescript and manuscript family histories and one-name studies.

(3)   Schools & Universities. Registers of public and other schools and of the ancient British universities and colleges. There is a published catalogue, *School, university and college registers and histories in the library of the Society of Genealogists* (1996; £3.50).

(4)   Apprentices of Great Britain 1710-1774. The record of the collection of the tax on apprenticeship indentures. In two alphabetical series 1710-1762 and 1762-1774, with indexes of the masters.

(5)   Professions. The series includes good runs of Army and Navy Lists and of the Medical Register with material on other professions arranged in alphabetical order. The maritime material here and elsewhere in the Library is listed in *Maritime sources in the library of the Society of Genealogists* (1997; £2.50).

(6)   Boyd's Marriage Index (described above, Section 10).

(7)   Heraldry, Royalty, Peerage, Biography. There are extensive runs of Burke's Peerage and Burke's Landed Gentry, Debrett's Peerage, Walford's County Families, and the older peerages.

(8)   Religions. Includes a run of Crockford's Clerical Directory, material on the various nonconformist denominations, the publications of the Catholic Record Society, the Huguenot Society, the Jewish Historical Society and other related works.

(9)   Wills. Many indexes of wills are located in the Middle Library but those which cover more than one county are here. The Society has indexes for nearly all the ancient probate courts in England and Wales from the sixteenth century or earlier to 1858, many on microfilm. They are described in *Will indexes and other probate material in the library of the Society of Genealogists* (1996; £9.25).

(10) Marriage Licences. Many indexes of marriage licences are located in the Middle Library but those which cover more than one county are here. See *Marriage licences: abstracts and indexes in the library of the Society of Genealogists* (4th edn. 1991).

(11) Genealogical periodicals and Public Records.

(12) Overseas. Collections of material on British people living abroad, in the Commonwealth and in America, are maintained. They include many

indexes of passenger lists of people going to America before 1900. Periodicals are received from numerous genealogical societies worldwide. Material on the British in India is listed in *Sources for Anglo-Indian genealogy in the library of the Society of Genealogists* (1990; £0.90).

(c) **Lower Library**: In the two rooms on the ground floor there is a microfilm collection of nearly 6,500 reels and much microfiche material, the main items being as follows:

(1) General Register Office, indexes of births, marriages and deaths in England and Wales 1837-1920, on microfiche.

(2) Indexes of births, marriages and deaths in Scotland, 1855-1920, on microfilm, and complete indexes of baptisms and marriages before 1855 on microfiche.

(3) International Genealogical Index. The 1992 edition on microfiche with 187 million baptisms and marriages worldwide including events at sea. The most recent edition on CD-ROM is available in the Middle Library where advance booking is necessary.

(4) Principal Probate Registry, microfilm indexes of wills and administrations for England and Wales 1858-1930.

(5) The Times, indexes of births, marriages and deaths reported in *The Times* 1785-1933 (with the announcements themselves to 1920) on microfilm. There are yearly manuscript indexes to the deaths 1894-1931 and a typescript index to divorces reported in *The Times* 1780-1910, in the Upper Library.

(6) Bernau Index. An index on microfilm of Chancery and other Court proceedings containing about four and a half million references prior to 1800. See *How to use the Bernau index* (Society of Genealogists, 1996; £2.40).

(7) Indexes on microfiche of births, marriages and deaths in Australia (Tasmania is available on CD-ROM) to 1902 (later for some states) and in New Zealand 1848-1920.

(8) Microfiche, in alphabetical order by surname, of material received for the Document Collection (see above) since February 1992.

Also in the Lower Library are a great number of card indexes, including a miscellaneous slip index, known as the Great Card Index, with about three million references, mainly relating to London and the South East of England prior to 1800 but containing a wide variety of other material.

The Society actively organises and encourages the transcription of parish registers and monumental inscriptions and seeks to provide a clearing house for information on the whereabouts of copies of both.

The Society has a bookshop with a wide range of genealogical and related books which is also worth visiting. This is open Monday, Tuesday, Friday & Saturday 10.00-6.00 and Wednesday & Thursday 10.00-8.00. For up-to-date lists of Society publications, bookshop stock, or microfiche and maps for sale, send a stamped addressed envelope or two International Reply Coupons.

13
COUNTY RECORD OFFICES AND LIBRARIES

When you have exhausted the records of civil registration and census returns and have begun to look at the parish registers of the area from which your family came you will need to consult the other sources available in the county record office.

Each county has at least one county record office supported by the local authority. It may have a close connection with a local studies library. Like county libraries the record offices are open without charge, though fees are charged in the offices at Exeter, Gloucester and Lincoln. When visiting a library or record office for the first time always contact it in advance to make sure that they have the records you require, to check the opening hours and, when necessary, to book a seat or a microfilm or microfiche reader. Evidence of identity and address or a reader's ticket may be required. If a guide to the office's contents has been published this will make a good starting point so that when you go you have a clear idea of what searches you intend to carry out. If you have several alternative research strategies you will not then be disappointed to have gone a long way only to find that you do not have sufficient things to occupy your time. When visiting or writing to a record office please bear in mind the points made in Section 17 below.

The main records used by genealogists in county record offices are:

(1) Census returns (see above, Section 8). The copies found locally are listed in J. Gibson, *Census returns 1841-1891 on microfilm* (FFHS, 6th edn. 1994; £2.50).

(2) Parish registers (see above, Section 10). The county record office will always have the latest details of the whereabouts of any register in the county. Copies are now normally seen on microfilm or microfiche and in a few counties are available through the local county library system. Also at the record office will be the annual copies of the parish registers called 'bishops' transcripts' and the local licences issued for marriages, both of which may provide variant or additional material.

(3) Other parish records, varying in quantity but perhaps including the accounts of churchwardens and of the overseers of the poor and papers about the legal place of 'settlement' of poor people. There may also be workhouse records and, after 1834, records of the Poor Law Unions.

(4) Wills proved in the local church courts before 1858. See J. Gibson, *Probate jurisdictions: where to look for wills* (FFHS, 4th edn. 1994; £3.50). Do not forget to consult the indexes to the wills proved in the Prerogative Court of Canterbury as well (see below, Section 15).

(5) The records of the administration of the county will include Land Tax records showing owners and occupiers, at least from 1780. See J. Gibson, *Quarter session records for family historians* (FFHS, 4th edn. 1995; £2.50).

(6) Record offices and some larger libraries may have files of electoral registers perhaps going back to 1832, arranged by street and not by name.

(7) Directories. Trade directories were published in many towns from the 1770s onwards and for country areas from the 1820s. They may help to locate a family in the Census Returns.

(8) Newspapers. Sets of local newspapers may be found in county record offices or libraries. Only a few are indexed by name. If they cannot be seen locally there will be copies at the British Library Newspaper Library, Colindale Avenue, London NW9 5HE (tel. 0171 412 7353). See J. Gibson, *Local newspapers 1750-1920: a select location list* (FFHS, 1991). Large reference libraries may have *The Times* on microfilm, together with its printed indexes. These indexes do not include the reported births, marriages and deaths and for indexes to these see Section 12 above.

(9) Maps. Many local libraries and record offices have early editions of Ordnance Survey maps or will know where copies of the six inch to the mile maps may be seen. Record offices may have other manuscript maps including Enclosure Awards showing fields and commons in the eighteenth and nineteenth centuries and Tithe Maps (between 1836 and 1860), both providing the names of owners and occupiers of land.

(10) Schools. The existence of a local school can be ascertained from the brief descriptions of villages found in trade directories and if its registers survive they will be at the school or at the county record office. Universal elementary education did not start until 1870 and even after that date it seems that more log books of incidental events survive than registers of pupils.

(11) Apprentices. The drawing up of apprenticeship indentures involved trouble and expense and most working children were trained without such formality. To make matters worse indentures were private documents and most have not survived. Those indentures which were taxed are recorded in a series of ledgers at the Public Record Office, Kew, 1710-1808, but do not show parentage after about 1750. There are indexes 1710-1774 at the Society of Genealogists. At county record offices one may find some record of poor apprentices paid for by their parishes between 1601 and 1834 or by some local charity and in borough record offices there may be a record of apprentices in a company or guild or in the borough itself.

(12) Records of local land or estate owners and of local businesses.

A useful book giving much practical information about visiting record offices is J. Cole & R. Church, *In and around record repositories in Great Britain and Ireland* (Family Tree Magazine, 3rd edn. 1992). Addresses and opening hours are given in the official *Record repositories in Great Britain* (PRO Publications, 10th edn. 1997; £3.99). An attempt to list the indexes of names to be found in county record offices is J. Gibson, *Unpublished personal name indexes in record offices and libraries* (FFHS, 2nd edn. 1987).

This booklet has only mentioned a few of the printed books which are of assistance to family historians and which are to be found in public libraries. An excellent survey of the wide variety available is R. Harvey, *Genealogy for librarians* (Library Association Publishing, London, 2nd edn. 1992).

Little of this material is available for home reading and so a certain amount of travelling will be inevitable though photocopies can sometimes be provided. There is no right to have photocopies and if this is likely to damage the book or manuscript or, indeed, to infringe copyright then the custodian has a responsibility to see that no photocopying is carried out.

14
LOCAL FAMILY HISTORY SOCIETIES

In addition to the Society of Genealogists there are many local family history societies. Membership of the one in your area and of those where your family came from may be helpful. They have regular meetings and talks, undertake valuable transcription and indexing work and produce quarterly journals and other publications. If you join one of these societies details of the families in which you are interested may usually be published in its journal without charge.

Many local societies have compiled indexes of marriages in their areas, of monumental inscriptions, census returns and other records. The societies will usually undertake postal searches in these indexes in return for small fees. These indexes and the fees charged are listed in J. Gibson & E. Hampson, *Marriage, census and other indexes for family historians* (Federation of Family History Societies, 6th edn. 1996; £3.50).

Some local societies have extensive publishing programmes of basic indexes and other material for their areas. Those works available are listed in two publications of the Federation of Family History Societies, *Current publications by member societies* (9th edn. 1997; £4.95) and *Current publications by member societies on microfiche* (4th edn. 1997; £4.95).

Although you may not have ancestors in the area where you now live there are several advantages in joining the local society. You will be able to see the exchange journals received from many other local societies not only in the British Isles but from overseas as well. There will also be a basic reference library and a bookstall as well as periodic lectures about sources in general.

As mentioned above (Section 4) full details of most societies worldwide, including subscription rates, will be found in the annually published *Genealogical research directory*.

The majority of the local family history societies in England and Wales and many overseas belong to the Federation of Family History Societies (FFHS) and an up-to-date list of addresses of these societies may be obtained from its Administrator, c/o Benson Room, Birmingham & Midland Institute, Margaret Street, Birmingham B3 3BS, and is published twice yearly in its journal *Family history news and digest* (subscription £4.60 for two issues, from Mr J.B. Rowlands, 18 Marine Terrace, Aberystwyth, Dyfed SY23 2AZ). The Federation itself has no library and does not undertake research. Details of local societies in Scotland may be obtained from the Scottish Association of Family History Societies, 51/3 Mortonhall Road, Edinburgh EH9 2HN.

15
PUBLIC RECORD OFFICE

The Public Record Office (PRO) houses the records of central government and the law courts from Domesday Book in 1086 to the present century. The staff do not undertake genealogical research.

The search rooms are located at the Public Record Office, Ruskin Avenue, Kew, Richmond, Surrey TW9 4DU (tel. 0181 876 3444) and are open to the public from 9.30 am to 5.00 pm, Monday to Saturday, except on public holidays and during the first two weeks of October.

A reader's ticket must be obtained in order to see original records and is issued on production of some positive means of identification, such as a banker's card, or, for foreign nationals, a passport or some other form of national identification document.

Many documents which refer to individuals are closed for 100 years in order to safeguard personal confidentiality and no public record is normally made available until thirty years after the date of its final creation.

All the material formerly in the old Public Record Office building in Chancery Lane (which has been closed) is now at Kew, but a group of records heavily used by genealogists have been made available in central London on the first floor of the Family Records Centre (see above, Sections 7 and 8). These consist mainly of microform copies of the census returns 1841-1891, the wills and administrations before 1858 from the Prerogative Court of Canterbury, the Estate Duty Office death duty registers 1796-1858 and the non-parochial registers 1567-1858. No reader's ticket is needed for the consultation of this material.

The main records used by genealogists at Kew are probably those of personnel in the services and professions. For further details see the guides mentioned below which should be consulted prior to any visit. They include:

(a) Army; see M.J. & C.T. Watts, *My ancestor was in the British Army* (Society of Genealogists, 1992, reprinted with an addenda 1995; £5.50); S. Fowler, *Army records for family historians* (PRO, 1992; £4.75) and S. Fowler, W. Spencer & S. Tamblin, *Army service records of the First World War* (PRO, 1996; £5.99).

(b) Navy; see N.A.M. Rodger, *Naval records for genealogists* (PRO, 1988; £4.95).

(c) Merchant seamen; see C.T. & M.J. Watts, *My ancestor was a merchant seaman* (Society of Genealogists, 1991; £4.60).

(d) Marines from 1793; see G. Thomas, *Records of the Royal Marines* (PRO, 1994; £8.95).

(e) Royal Air Force; see E. Wilson, *The records of the Royal Air Force: how to find The Few* (FFHS, 1991; £3.95) and S. Fowler, P. Elliott, R.C. Nesbit & C. Goulter, *R.A.F. records in the Public Record Office* (PRO, 1994; £8.95).

(f) Coastguards from 1816 to 1923.

(g) Customs officers from 1683 and excisemen from 1696.

(h) Metropolitan Police from 1829 (except 1857-1869); see L.A. Waters, *Police history monograph: notes for family historians* (Police History Society, 1987).

(i) Railway staff registers from 1835; see T. Richards, *Was your grandfather a railwayman?* (FFHS, 3rd edn. 1995; £4.95) and D.T. Hawkings, *Railway ancestors: a guide to the staff records of the railway companies of England and Wales 1822-1947* (PRO & Sutton Publishing, 1995; £25).

(j) Solicitors' articles of clerkship 1730-1875.

(k) Clergy institutions to benefices 1556-1838.

Records of postmen 1737-1940 are not at the Public Record Office but at the Post Office Archives, Freeling House, Mount Pleasant, London EC1A 1BB (tel. 0171 239 2570); see J. Farrugia, *A guide to the Post Office archives* (1987).

Records of civil and criminal litigation are also held at Kew. For these the general guide mentioned below should be consulted but for criminals see also D.T. Hawkings, *Criminal ancestors; a guide to historical criminal records in England and Wales* (Sutton Publishing, 1996; £14.99).

First-time visitors to the Public Record Office are strongly advised to read J. Cox, *New to Kew?* (PRO, 1997; £5.99) but for fuller details see A. Bevan and A. Duncan, *Tracing your ancestors in the Public Record Office* (HMSO, 4th edn. 4th impression 1995; £7.95) and S. Colwell, *Dictionary of genealogical sources in the Public Record Office* (1992).

16
FAMILY HISTORY CENTRES

Family History Centres are branches of the Family History Library in Salt Lake City, Utah. They are usually located in the meeting houses of the Church of Jesus Christ of Latter-Day Saints but are open without charge or formality to any member of the public.

Each centre has copies of the International Genealogical Index (see above, Section 10) and the Family History Library Catalogue, i.e. the catalogue of the library in Salt Lake City. If the centre has the International Genealogical Index on computer as part of the group of programs called 'FamilySearch' it will normally also have the program called 'Ancestral File' which contains details of a further 29 million people linked in 11 million families. Many of the latter will be American. Another section of FamilySearch which is of great value in tracing families in America is the Social Security Death Index which provides details of over 50 million people who have died in America since 1937. The centres may also have reference sources and copies of some records.

At these centres it is possible to carry out a remarkable range of research by borrowing microfilm or microfiche copies of records from Salt Lake City, chosen from the Family History Library Catalogue. A small fee is charged. Thus, if you have ancestors or family, for instance, in Germany or America you may be able to see the records involved without the necessity of going to those countries. The scope of the records held can be seen from J. Cerny and E. Elliott, *The library: a guide to the LDS Family History Library* (Ancestry Publishing, Salt Lake City, 1988).

The centres are staffed by volunteers and they vary in their opening hours. A list of those in the British Isles may be obtained from the British Isles Family History Service Centre, 399 Garretts Green Lane, Birmingham B33 0UH. The address of your nearest centre will be found in *The phone book* under 'Church of Jesus Christ of Latter-Day Saints'. Always telephone in advance to check opening hours; the centres will not normally answer inquiries by post.

17
SOME WORDS OF ADVICE

It has been truly said that genealogy is basically a do-it-yourself pastime. You may be lucky and discover relatives who are tracing the same lines and who are willing to share their information but the greatest satisfaction comes from the slow assemblage of facts over a period of time and from personal research.

A family history is not something which can be put together in a few months, let alone a few weeks or hours. It may take a good deal of time. Success will depend to a large extent on the social status of the family you are tracing, on the frequency of its surname, on the way in which it moves about and changes its occupation and, inevitably, on the extent to which the appropriate records have survived. Many genealogists, it has to be said, encounter problems in the nineteenth century and are immediately discouraged.

However, although your family may be uniquely interesting the problems you have in tracing it will be the same as those of any other genealogist. That is why reading about the subject in different textbooks and meeting other genealogists through your local family history society can be very worthwhile.

It is not fair, however, to expect librarians and record office staff to take a personal interest in your searches however intensely interesting and exciting they may be. There are many thousands of genealogists and they have put a great strain on the services and goodwill of archivists and librarians, not only in the British Isles but worldwide. Lengthy letters, telephone calls and conversation may be met with polite interest but please remember that they detract from the main work of any office.

Always, therefore, keep any letter of enquiry as short as possible and make sure, before you send it, that the answer is not easily available by personal visit to your local public library. This is where access to the library and bookstall of your local family history society can be so useful.

It is also well to remember, when asking for information from anyone, private or official, that there may be no reply unless you provide an addressed envelope with appropriate stamps (or, for correspondents abroad, International Reply Coupons obtainable from Post Offices).

18
PROFESSIONAL ASSISTANCE

If you yourself are not in a position to trace your family, or if you need help in distant parts of the United Kingdom, or with documents in Latin or a difficult handwriting, there are professional searchers who undertake such work.

The Association of Genealogists and Record Agents (AGRA) was founded in 1968 to promote high standards among professional genealogists. The Association publishes an annual *List of members* showing the geographical and subject areas of their expertise. This is available from the Society of Genealogists (£2.50 including postage) which also publishes a leaflet, *Employing a professional researcher: a practical guide* (Leaflet 28, 1997; £0.25).

A list of professionals in Scotland may be obtained from the Association of Scottish Genealogists and Record Agents (ASGRA), PO Box 174, Edinburgh EH3 5QZ, and in Ireland from the Association of Professional Genealogists in Ireland (APGI), 2 Kildare Street, Dublin 2, Eire.

INDEX

References are to Sections, not pages